HOW TO BUILD BOUNDARIES

Metropolitan Youssef

ST MARY & MOSES ABBEY PRESS

How to Build Boundaries
By Metropolitan Youssef

Designed & Published by:
St. Mary & St. Moses Abbey Press
101 S Vista Dr, Sandia, TX 78383
stmabbeypress.com

Translation from Arabic by St. Mary & St. Moses Abbey.

Contents

Introduction

We may liken boundaries to a fence that has gates, which are opened to let everything good in, [but] are closed to whatever is bad so that they may not sneak in to us. If I purchase a piece of land, for example, I would build a fence around it, so that I may declare that whatever is within this fence falls under my charge—because I own it—and whatever is outside [this fence] does not fall under my charge—because I do not own it. Likewise, also, when I set boundaries in place for my life, I open my heart to whatever is good, and close it to whatever is bad. So, if I closed shut my heart completely, and did not let it ever be opened, this fence is [consequently] transformed into a mere wall that completely isolates and imprisons me.

Having boundaries is not against love and individuality. They make clear our responsibilities and our role, and Holy Scripture teaches us that the Holy Trinity is One: Trinity in One, and One in Trinity. Despite the existence of perfect love among the Hypostases of the Holy Trinity, there is distinction among them even in responsibilities.

An example of this is when the disciples asked the Lord Christ [at a time] near His ascension to heaven: "Therefore, when they had come together, they asked Him, saying, 'Lord, will You at this time restore the kingdom to Israel?' And He said to them, 'It is not for you to know times and seasons which the Father has put in His own authority.'"[1] The word "in His authority" means within His boundaries and within the domain of His responsibility. The Lord Christ also said, "For the Father judges no one, but has committed all judgment to the Son."[2] That is, the responsibility of the Son, and His authority, is the judgment of the world, because it is the Son who was incarnate and became Man, and became a "merciful and faithful High Priest" as St. Paul the Apostle characterized Him in [the Epistle to the] Hebrews[3]. He was like us in everything except for sin, and consequently He is able to judge us. And also, concerning the Holy Spirit, "the Spirit of truth who proceeds from the Father,"[4] this procession is from the Father, and consequently, we cannot say that this procession is from the Father and the Son, because by this, I do not distinguish the boundaries among the Hypostases.

---

1   Acts 1:6–7.
2   John 5:22.
3   Hebrews 2:17.
4   John 15:26.

And so, we see that, despite the existence of love among the three Hypostases, and despite that They are One, there are boundaries and distinction, and this is not in opposition to love and oneness. There are many verses making it clear how the Lord Christ put boundaries in many matters. For example, when they said to Him that "everyone is looking for You"; "but He said to them, 'Let us go into the next towns, that I may preach there also, because for this purpose I have come forth.'"[5] Also, when they were pressing Him to teach them and preach to them, the Scripture says: "So He Himself often withdrew into the wilderness and prayed."[6] All this means that the Lord Christ—glory be to Him—used to put boundaries for Himself in His relationship with people, and also in His relationship with the Father in His prayers. He did not let people have control over His time and His responsibilities.

---

5   Mark 1:38.
6   Luke 5:16.

1

Types of Personalities

Problems we encounter arise when we do not know how to build sound boundaries with others. The other [person] has an identity and a personality distinct from mine. People may be divided into four types of personalities based on their issues related to boundaries with others.

The First Type: The Compliant

These do not know [how] to say "No," but say "Yes" always, to the good and the bad. Were they to answer [with a "Yes"] to the good things, no problem would there be, but they open the door to the bad things also, which cause them harm. And those are they who were taught by their parents, when they were young, that it is wrong to say "No" because the children of Christ do not say "No," even though the Lord Christ [Himself] said to us, "But let your

'Yes' be 'Yes,' and your 'No,' 'No.'"[7] This means that there is a time in which I must say "Yes," and a time in which I must say "No." Therefore, they[8] have not learned to say "No" when someone takes advantage of them, have not learned to say "No" to the enticements of sin, or when someone controls them, or when someone allures them or deceives them, as the serpent deceived our mother Eve.

God has granted us [the option] to say "No" as a weapon to protect us from being taken advantage of, from enticements, from being wrongly controlled by others, and also from deception. Imagine, had Joseph the Righteous not known [how] to say "No" to Potiphar's wife, what would have become of his life and his eternity? Had our fathers the martyrs not known [how] to say "No" to worshiping idols, and had St. Athanasius not known [how] to say "No" when Arius spoke [falsely] about the Lord Christ that He is less than the Father, what would have become of our faith?

There are times when it is necessary that we say "No," but the problem of the compliant is that they always say "Yes," and cannot say "No." Therefore, we have to, as fathers, Sunday School servants, and counseling servants, teach our children to say "No" at certain times. And they should not feel ashamed to say "No," because this protects them from the world

---

7   Matthew 5:37.

8   i.e. the compliant.

which is full of evil, sin, exploitation[9], controlling, and deception.

The problem for the compliant may be more serious than this. Not only are they unable to say "No," they are also unable to identify the bad things; they cannot distinguish between what is good and what is bad, because this requires a [certain] level of spiritual maturity, for it is completely not easy to distinguish between what is good and what is bad, especially in ambiguous matters. Our teacher Paul the Apostle says:

> For everyone who partakes only of milk is unskilled in the word of righteousness, for he is a babe. But solid food belongs to those who are of full age, that is, those who by reason of use have their senses exercised to discern both good and evil.[10]

He called them "those who are of full age," that is, those who are spiritually mature.

Our mother Eve thought that eating of the tree of the knowledge of good and evil, was a good thing because she was unable to distinguish between a good thing and bad thing. So she was persuaded by the words of the devil who said to her, "For God knows that in the day you eat of it your eyes will be

---

9   i.e. being taken advantage of.
10   Hebrews 5:13–14.

opened, and you will be like God, knowing good and evil."[11] Because she thought that it was a good thing to be like God, she ate of the tree; and not only did she eat, but she also gave her husband [to eat].

The compliant are not only unable to say "No," but they also do not perceive what is bad. I would like to make this clear through [relating] a story of a lady whose manager used to give her extra work which took time at the expense of her home and children. She could not say "No" because she did not see this as a bad thing. She used to perform the responsibilities of her friend who would spend long hours on the phone in trivial conversations. She could not say "No," but on the contrary, she considered what she was doing as a sort of sacrifice, giving and patience. By this, she let every person exploit her by using verses from Holy Scriptures like, "For even the Son of Man did not come to be served, but to serve,"[12] even though the Lord Christ [Himself] said "No" when the situation demanded , and as we have previously mentioned that He said "No" to the multitudes that asked Him to stay with them: "I must go to other cities."[13]

[Some] of the reasons making a person lose the ability to say "No," [are the following]:

---

11   Genesis 3:5.

12   Mark 10:45.

13   See Mark 1:38 and Luke 4:43.

1. The fear of hurting the feelings of others

Since he does not want to hurt the feelings of the other person, he continues to always say "Yes," even though he may not have the ability to give. Nevertheless, if he has the ability to give and [if it is] within the domain of his responsibility, in this case, he sins if he says "No."

Therefore, it is important for the priests to realize, regarding the youth, that there is a difference between a person who falls into sin because of his weakness and his inability to say "No," and another [person] who falls into sin because of his negligence. The wise father of confession has to distinguish between them; so he may help the first person and toughen him to say "No" to sin, as Joseph said, "How then can I do this great wickedness, and sin against God?"[14] As for the second [person], the saying of Paul the Apostle is fitting for him, "Therefore 'put away from yourselves the evil person.'"[15] This person might need that the Church take a stand regarding him, because he lives in insolence. Both have made a mistake and fallen into the same sin, yet the father of confession must realize what [lies] behind the sin. Is it a weakness, because he cannot say "No" to the enticement of sin? And consequently, here the person needs help, support and encouragement, as

---

14   Genesis 39:9.

15   1 Corinthians 5:13.

Paul the Apostle says, "Comfort[16] the fainthearted, uphold the weak, be patient with all."[17] But if the cause of sin is insolence, the treatment is different in this case.

2. The fear of losing the love of people

Sometimes when some people hear the word "No" [said to them], they shun the person who said it and stop dealing with him. Thus, this person feels that he has lost the love of these people, and his relationship with them has come to an end. Consequently, the fear of losing the relationship and the love makes the person unable to say "No." Therefore, he has to examine himself, because he is giving not out of love, but out of fear.

> *"If you want no sorrow to befall you, make no one sorrowful."*
>
> —St. John Chrysostom—

3. The fear of the reaction of the other

Some people's reaction may be anger, agitation, and [even] rage sometimes; therefore, he complies always to avoid their anger, and he lives in peace and does not stir up problems with them. Obedience, here,

---

16   Or: encourage.
17   1 Thessalonians 5:14.

emanates out the fear of the others' anger.

A person might fear that he might be punished if he said "No," as the case was with the worker whom we have spoked about previously. She did not say "No" and took [extra] work home with her, which she was given by her manager or one of her friends. This was at the expense of her time with her children and her husband and her responsibilities at home. It made her stay up late, sleeping at a late hour. It was likely that her manager might have penalized[18] her, had she refused. The motive here is the fear of punishment or of the damage that may have befallen her.

4. The fear of losing the nice image

A person may also think that if he said "No," people will say that he is not spiritual or is not a person inclined to giving. When a new church is being built, for example, this person may be asked to donate for this purpose, so he pays, not out of love for giving, but so that others may not say that he is selfish or not spiritual. He donates[19] in pursuit of the praise of people and the glorification of the ego, and not because of his love for, and obedience to, God. And thus, he will not be able to say "No," to keep the beautiful idol he made for himself; he

---

18   Or: punished.
19   Literally: pays.

wants to preserve his image before people.

5. The feeling of guilt

There are people who always say "Yes" because they feel guilty. For example, in an exam, an acquaintance of one of the students may help him, that is, "help him cheat." Cheating here is wrong; therefore, he feels guilty if he does not help others, and consequently his conscience reproaches him regarding the things that are wrong. Judas Iscariot, also, returned the thirty [pieces] of silver because of his feeling of guilt. But his feeling of guilt did not spring from God and [was not] a result of the work of the Holy Spirit; therefore, Paul the Apostle mentions that there is a sorrow according to the will of God and a sorrow according to the world, saying, "For godly sorrow produces repentance leading to salvation, not to be regretted; but the sorrow of the world produces death."[20] The person has to differentiate between the feeling of guilt that is from God and the work of the Holy Spirit, and the one that originates from something else, like the ego.

There is a difference between the feeling of guilt or sorrow which is the work of the Holy Spirit and [that which stems from] a guilt complex. The guilt complex is that you reprove yourself of things of which the Holy Spirit does not reprove you, and

---

20   2 Corinthians 7:10.

this means that your conscience has a greater power over you than God. The Apostle Paul described it as a weak conscience, saying, "Their conscience, being weak, is defiled."[21] He also says, "Receive one who is weak in the faith, but not to disputes over doubtful things. For one believes he may eat all things, but he who is weak eats only vegetables."[22] Paul the Apostle is here speaking about the weak conscience which reproves a person of things God does not reprove him. There are people who forbid eating meats and consider that a sin, for when they started eating meats, their conscience would reprove them and trouble them, so they decided not to eat meats but only vegetables. This was because of the weak conscience; therefore, Paul the Apostle said, "But he who is weak eats only vegetables." And this is completely different from what we practice during the holy Great Fast. We refrain from eating meats, not because it is a sin—for we eat it on feasts and during the Holy Fifty [period]—but we refrain from eating meats so that the person may train himself: "But I discipline my body and bring it into subjection, lest, when I have preached to others, I myself should become disqualified."[23]

The Church intensely resisted those who forbid eating meats, and those who forbade marriage and marital relations. They abstain from marriage, not

---

21   1 Corinthians 8:7.

22   Romans 14:1–2.

23   1 Corinthians 9:27.

out of love for virginity and chastity, but because of the weak conscience. Choosing virginity out of love for God is a different thing. Therefore, the Apostle Paul spoke of this subject, saying:

> Let the husband render to his wife the affection due her, and likewise also the wife to her husband. The wife does not have authority over her own body, but the husband does. And likewise the husband does not have authority over his own body, but the wife does. Do not deprive one another except with consent for a time, that you may give yourselves to fasting and prayer; and come together again so that Satan does not tempt you because of your lack of self-control.[24]

The Apostle Paul, here, dealt with the idea of forbidding marriage and sexual relations between the husband and wife, and also [forbidding] eating meats. If one side abstained from marital relations, this is because of his feeling of guilt or because his conscience is weak. The Apostle Paul looked at it as defilement, saying, "Their conscience, being weak, is defiled."[25] It[26] also defiles the person. For

---

24   1 Corinthians 7:3–5.

25   1 Corinthians 8:7.

26   i.e. the weak conscience.

keeping[27] the commandments mentioned in Holy Scriptures is an obedience because of love for God, and not because of fear. As to the outward obedience which is accompanied by inward grumbling, it is not obedience at all. When you obey—while grumbling, objecting, and being discontented with what you are doing—you are lying to yourself and to others. As to true obedience, it originates from within.

Yes, in this obedience there may be a sort of forcing oneself and endurance, but there is in it conviction also, as it happened with Abraham when he obeyed God, to slay his son Isaac. This was not, of course, an easy thing for him [to obey], but it was also an obedience from within, before it being one from without. [There is] a difference between the obedience which comes with a struggle and forcing oneself, and the outward obedience which is accompanied by inward grumbling as a result of me disagreeing and objecting because I am afraid and cannot say "No," or because I have a guilt complex, or because I am afraid of hurting somebody else, or so that I may preserve my image before people. This [latter] obedience is not acceptable before God.

And in this manner I have to fulfill all the commandments. For example, the Lord Christ said, "But whoever slaps you on your right cheek, turn the other to him also."[28] So, if I turned the other

---

27 Or: obeying.
28 Matthew 5:39.

cheek out of fear, because I could not face the person who slapped me, saying to him, "Why did you slap me?"—this will be [considered] a vice, and not a virtue. But if I turned the other cheek because of my love for God, this will be [considered] a virtue, because the person, who is afraid of those who slap him on the right cheek, turning the other to them, will deny his faith if they asked me to do so. But the person who turns the other cheek because of his love for God will never deny his faith if he is asked to do so. This is what happened with the Lord Christ who had to say to the Jews, "Which of you convicts Me of sin?"[29] Because if they had blamed Him for a sin, He would have been a blemished Lamb, and His sacrifice would not have redeemed the world. Therefore, it was essential that He proves at the time of the trial that He is without sin and unblemished, for His sacrifice to be acceptable. When the servant of the high priest struck Him with his hands, "Jesus answered him, 'If I have spoken evil, bear witness of the evil; but if well, why do you strike Me?'"[30] After the trial was ended and Pontius Pilate delivered Him [to be crucified], however, the soldiers struck him with their hands, as Isaiah prophesied about Him: "I gave My back to those who struck Me, and My cheeks to those who plucked out the beard; I did not hide My face from shame and spitting."[31] When

---

29   John 8:46.

30   John 18:23.

31   Isaiah 50:6.

He left His cheeks open to those who smite[32], here, it was not out of weakness or inability to say "No;" He delivered Himself with His own entire will to the errors of others. Therefore, I have to differentiate, here, between whether my bearing insults and harm from others is due to my weakness, or due to my love for God: "Blessed are you when they revile and persecute you, and say all kinds of evil against you falsely for My sake."[33]

Every person can say "No" to abuse[34], evil, sin, and enticement; and he is able, with his entire will and choosing, to allow others to hurt him for God's sake. He endures insults even though he can stop this evil.

The Second Type: The Avoider

These are they who say "No" to good things, so they close shut their doors to them. As for the compliant, they open their doors to bad things. For example, the avoiders may have a need, and yet they refuse to ask others for help, and when others offer help, they refuse it. They shut their doors before what is good. They have a wrong understanding of "independence," for the person cannot live independently from the world surrounding him. The monastic fathers gave a definition, by divine wisdom, to this matter; so we

---

32   See Divine Liturgy According to St. Gregory – Holy Holy Holy.
33   Matthew 5:11.
34   Or: exploitation.

read in the Paradise of the Holy Fathers[35]: One of the fathers went to a spiritual elder and asked him, "Can I live, father, in a self-sufficient manner of life, so that I do not give anything to anybody nor do I take anything from anybody?" So the spiritual elder answered him, saying, "If you refuse to give, you lose love, and if you refuse to take, you lose humility."

There are two reasons behind refusing to accept help: the first is pride or the false self-honor, and the second is the feeling of unworthiness of receiving help from others, because he is inferior to others. And this [latter] is not out of humility; rather, it is out of weakness and faintheartedness.

The word "one other" recurs in the New Testament more than fifty times, some of which: "A new commandment I give to you, that you love one another; as I have loved you, that you also love one another."[36] "Bear one another's burdens, and so fulfill the law of Christ."[37] "Confess your trespasses to one another, and pray for one another, that you may be healed."[38] "In honor giving preference to one another."[39] "Therefore, receive one another, just

---

35 Literally: the Paradise of the Monks; this is the translation of the Arabic title.

36 John 13:34.

37 Galatians 6:2.

38 James 5:16.

39 Romans 12:10.

as Christ also received us, to the glory of God."[40]

All these verses, and others [more], make clear our responsibility toward one another. God has given me gifts[41] so that I may use them to serve others, as He has given others gifts so that they may use them to serve me. You need me, and I also need you. You depend on me, and I also depend on you. So if I isolate myself from others and accept help from no one, this is against the law of God. When God created Adam, He said: "And the LORD God said, 'It is not good that man should be alone; I will make him a helper comparable to him.'"[42]

The person who lives in isolation from others and refrains from helping others, has a problem with boundaries, because he shuts his doors to good things, as though he were unable to fully understand the word, "Yes, I am present here so that I may help you."

Nevertheless, we pray in the Divine Liturgy, "He made us unto Himself an assembled people, and sanctified us."[43]

[Why do the avoiders refuse help?]

1. Pride

---

40   Romans 15:7.

41   Or: talents.

42   Genesis 2:18.

43   See Divine Liturgy According to St. Basil – Holy Holy Holy.

The avoiders do not allow [both] the good and the bad from entering, even though there may be a risk that God may be left[44] outside the heart, and he does not allow Him to come in: "Behold, I stand at the door and knock. If anyone hears My voice and opens the door, I will come in to him and dine with him, and he with Me."[45]

When the Holy Scripture said, "Rachel weeping for her children, refusing to be comforted, because they are no more,"[46] it was not talking about Rachel, the mother of Joseph and Benjamin, but it is a prophecy[47] of the mothers of the children of Bethlehem. What I would like to emphasize here is that she is "refusing to be comforted;" that is, she shuts her heart to being comforted[48]. This also is what happens when a person loses someone dear to him, and [while] the Holy Spirit is ready to fill his heart with comfort, but he shuts his heart and refuses to be comforted. He has shut his heart to what is good, even though God encourages us, because He knows our needs and satisfies them.

There is nothing wrong in a person to know his needs and satisfy them. And this is what the Lord did with Adam, as we have previously mentioned; therefore, God made us within families, gave us

---

44   Literally: present.

45   Revelation 3:20.

46   Matthew 2:18.

47   Literally: symbolize.

48   Literally: to comfort, to consolation.

friends, commanded us to worship Him through a church, through a gathered congregation, because relationships are very important for the safety of the person. The greater number of sound relationships does a person have, the more does this help him also to have sound psychological growth.

> *"Do not consent in your thoughts, nor characterize in your words, any person as evil. The Lord has loosened us from the bondage of the devil, so that we should not bind ourselves again nor give our souls up to slavery by our ill opinion."*

—St. Macarius—

2. Unworthiness

As to the second reason that makes the avoiders refuse accepting the help [offered them], and consequently refuse the good things, it is the feeling of unworthiness, which is also an inferiority complex. There is a difference between inferiority complex and humility. Inferiority complex is the feeling that I am less than others and am unworthy, while humility is the feeling that I am less than others but the grace of God lifts me up. "He raises the poor man from the earth and lifts up the poor from the dunghill so as to seat him with rulers, with the rulers of His people."[49]

The fact that God has given me grace does not mean that I deserve it. Humility focuses on the grace of God, for the person is poor but the grace of God lifts him up from the dunghill. As for the person who has inferiority complex, he is poor on the dunghill continually. This poor person, who is on the dunghill, may be both a compliant and avoider. He is suffering from a compound problem: he serves and helps everyone, but he refuses to be helped by anyone. He permits all people to take advantage of him, yet he says that this is love and service. He shuts his door to what is good, and opens it to every bad thing, because he feels that he is on a dunghill. He often shuts his door even to God Himself, as we have previously mentioned.

Therefore, we advise that when the priests, Sunday school servants, and those working in the field of counseling, speak about humility and unworthiness, they have to also speak about the grace of God. Otherwise, we would be raising generations that have a feeling of inferiority. There are many wives who bear with insults, beatings, and slurs from their husbands, because they consider themselves worthy of such a treatment. This undoubtedly is not a virtue, because such actions coming from their husbands are wrong, and they should work on putting an end to them.

49   Psalms 112:7–8 LXX, OSB.

The Third Type: The Dominating and Authoritarian

These people are the most difficult type to have problems with boundaries. These who have controlling personalities push open others' doors by force. They do not respect the others' boundaries; they do not take a "No" for an answer. No one can say "No" to them; unless he [is ready] to suffer hardships and for problems to be stirred up against him. They have a strange philosophy with which they interpret that the word "No" means to them "Maybe," or it may even be a "Yes;" and by this, the word "No" becomes "Yes." They, also, employ two methods to control others.

The first method is what we call hostility, [involving] anger, agitation, raised voice, threatening, severe punishments. These are the violent authoritarians.

The second method is deception, playing with emotions, making others feel guilty, and then they do what they want. These are the deceptive authoritarians.

The majority of the controlling men employ violence to control others, while the majority of the controlling women employ deception and shrewdness to have control.

This is what the serpent did with our mother Eve, for it beguiled her through trickery and cunning.

This is what we pray in the Divine Liturgy: "When we disobeyed Your commandment by the deceit of the serpent..."[50] One of the fathers said, "The devil controls the world by trickery, and if the devil were to lose his ability to deceive and trick the world, he would lose his control [as well]."

A mother, for example, may say to her son, "I got diabetes because you want to join the monastery." She wants to make him feel guilty, and then control him and exercise dominion over him.

The real problem, which those using the method of deception to control others have, is that they deny being controlling, and this is [so] because they adopt a manner that is gentle[51]; therefore, their case is difficult. We know that the case is difficult when the person denies that he has a problem. Addiction is not a problem of its own, because, if the person admits that he is an addict, he will begin searching for treatment. If he says, however, that there is no problem, because I can stop taking drugs at any time, he will not succeed, and it will be difficult to deal with him.

> *"The strong [person] is not he who defeats his enemy; rather, the strong is he who wins him."*
>
> —H.H. Pope Shenouda III—

---

50   See Divine Liturgy According to St. Basil – Holy Holy Holy.

51   Or: soft.

27

The Fourth Type: The Indolent

These are they who do not fulfill their responsibilities so as to meet the needs of others. A father, for example, may not want to do his role, so he does not provide for his home, even though this thing is one of his main responsibilities toward his home; Likewise, a mother who does not care for her husband and children. A son may ask his father for his necessities, but the father, despite his ability to give him—but even it is his responsibility to give him—being indolent, does not respond positively to his needs. As the saying goes, "An ear of mud, and an ear of dough."[52] Also as the Book of Proverbs says, "Do not withhold good from those to whom it is due, when it is in the power of your hand to do so."[53]

One of the clear examples on this, is when you go to a governmental office to finish some paperwork. The clerk, who is supposed to help[54], would make you wait for a long time, and in the end, he would ask you to come back the following day, and he might repeat doing the same thing the following day. This is a kind of indolence, for he does not perform his responsibility toward others.

There are two reasons that make a person indolent, and these are:

---

52   i.e. talking to a brick wall or having an ear of cloth.
53   Proverbs 3:27.
54   Literally: who has the stamp.

1. Narcissism

Narcissism is that a person is drowning in satisfying his own desires and pleasures, without caring at all about the needs of others. You may see, for example, the clerk sipping tea, and smoking cigarettes, and conversing with his colleagues, and he does not want to be encumbered by his work, even though this is the time specified for work. He does not care about others and does not care if they are getting wearied or not. This behavior is contrary to the teaching of the Holy Scripture which says, "Let each of you look out not only for his own interests, but also for the interests of others."[55] This indolent person is suffering from a compound problem: If he asks for something, he wants all to do it for him, and woe to the person who objects and says "No;" yet, at the same time, he refuses to perform his responsibilities toward others.

This may happen also with some of the leading Church servants. For example, the service coordinator may want all the other servants to submit to him, and whoever says "No" is punished. At the same time, he refuses to submit to the priest. Such as person is dominating and indolent, because he wants to have dominion over others and refuses to perform his role or do his responsibility, and [part] of his responsibility is to be [himself] in submission as well. As for the person who has a

---

55 Philippians 2:4.

moderate[56] personality, he, before asking others to submit to him, presents himself as a role model in submission. The Lord Christ, before telling us to be obedient to Him, of whom Holy Scripture says, "became obedient to the point of death, even the death of the cross."[57] He obeyed the Father and gave His will up to Him[58] entirely.

2. The Spirit of Revenge on the Other

The second reason for indolence may be [the existence] of a high vengeful spirit against the needs of others. For example, when you ask a clerk to complete your request, he would say to you, "Wait until tomorrow. There is no problem for you to wait until tomorrow; or else, go to someone else to complete your request." This is a vengeful spirit, and it is the projection of his hatred to others' need in his life.

Our understanding of boundaries will help us realize how to deal, in an appropriate way, with the different personalities, and consequently, we can give them the appropriate advice. The cure for a person from anger which is due to the love of having control is different from the cure for a person from anger which is due to compliance. The compliant lacks the spirit of taking initiative and

---

56 That is, straight, not convoluted.

57 Philippians 2:8.

58 i.e. the Father.

needs someone else to lead him. There is one final advice: that we should not go too far in analyzing people, and should not work hard to label them as compliant, controlling, indolent, or avoider, because this will get us into big trouble. Here we are speaking about the field of service.

Work-related and Relationships-related Boundaries

Work-related boundaries are the boundaries that concern your job; they [refer to] the ability to perform our work in a manner pleasing to God and to our superiors. It concerns our ability to plan, take initiative, be orderly, and perform [our work]. The worker should be committed to going to work at the specified hour, coming back to his home on time; he is productive in his work, plans well, is serious in all his actions, fulfills his responsibilities by the appointed time, does not exhaust himself by bearing responsibilities greater than his power. Therefore, he is successful in his work. If he consents, however, to taking responsibilities greater than his ability, he would not execute them well. But the person, who builds boundaries in his work, will receive rewards, and will be promoted in his work, etc.

As to the relationships-related boundaries, they [refer to] the ability to establish relationships that are based on love and truth with others. As Paul the Apostle says, "Speaking the truth in love,"[59] so these

---

59   Ephesians 4:15.

two foundations are necessary, "love and truth," so that our relationships with others may prosper.

Some people may be successful in [establishing] the work-related boundaries, but fail in their relationships-related boundaries. So it may be said about someone that he is successful in his work, but is a failure in his social life, and vice versa. Our goal, as children of God, is to be successful in [both] the work-related and relationships-related boundaries.

> *"If you want to give people comfort, do so in a way they [themselves] find comforting to them, not according to your [own] thinking, because you may be trying to give them comfort in a manner that troubles them."*
>
> —H.H. Pope Shenouda III—

✝ ✝ ✝

2

How to Build Boundaries?

Some [people] may believe that, by merely reading this book, they will reach the point of perfection in building boundaries. This is not true. Here, we are presenting an understanding of boundaries so that we may realize and understand what sound and unsound boundaries are.

This understanding requires constant training and practical application. No one can build boundaries with another except by divine help, and by human help also, especially if he is working with a dominating or controlling personality, because every time he tries to build boundaries with this personality, he exposes himself to intense punishment. Without divine help, he will get more tired and will grumble more. Do not try to begin building boundaries wherein you may encounter some disagreements which you cannot face on your own, especially if you are of the compliant personalities.

Every person is able to obtain divine help through prayer and his relationship with God, through [reading] the Holy Scriptures, Church Mysteries[60], the attendance of Divine Liturgy and receiving Communion, spiritual guidance, and being filled with the Holy Spirit. As for human help, it comes through the father of confession and the servants, and through spiritual people who give him true guidance and who answer him truthfully.

This also applies to young children. To build boundaries with a young child and to teach him also how to build boundaries, I have to shower him with love first. This word is especially directed to fathers and mothers, that they should love their children and should let them feel this love, before teaching them how to build boundaries. So, if a father said to his son "No" when the son is not feeling the love of his father, he will think[61] that his father hates him and does not like him. Our teacher Paul the Apostle says, "That you, being rooted and grounded in love, may be able to comprehend with all the saints what is the width and length and depth and height."[62] So, the width and length and depth and height are boundaries, and I have to comprehend these boundaries, while being rooted in love, first.

---

60   Literally: the persistence in practicing Church Mysteries.

61   Or: interpret.

62   Ephesians 3:17–18.

The Stages of Building Boundaries

The first stage is what we call, the separation and individuality. An infant, within the scope of love, can distinguish himself from others, and can say, "Who I am and who I am not," as it happened with the Lord Christ when He was twelve years old. He remained, upon their return, in Jerusalem, without the knowledge of Joseph and His mother, and when they could not find Him, they returned back to Jerusalem looking for Him, so they found Him in the temple. His mother said to Him, "'Son, why have You done this to us?'... And He said to them, 'Why did you seek Me? Did you not know that I must be about My Father's business?'"[63] These are boundaries. The Lord Christ here said "No," for I am beginning the service for which I was sent from My Father. Had the Lord Christ not felt the love of Joseph the carpenter and the Virgin Mary, He would not have said these words to them. And had Joseph the carpenter and the Virgin Mary been of the controlling personalities, they would have punished their Son for leaving them. But the atmosphere that is filled with love is what made the Lord Christ say these words to them. Terms used here may be inappropriate—that is, Joseph the carpenter and the Virgin Mary punishing the Lord Christ—but our intention here is to talk about a father and mother punishing their child.

---

63   Luke 2:48–49.

35

For me to discover "who I am," I must discover "who I am not." For example, before purchasing a piece of land, I have to question its border lines. Children pass through three stages to build sound boundaries:

1. The Distinction Stage

When a baby is born, he is tightly bound to his mother, because he had been in his mother's womb for nine months, and he and his mother are one. His comprehension develops, however, and he grows up year after another, until he learns that he and his mother are not one. And this is the stage of the building of boundaries. Thus, the child begins separating himself gradually from his mother, and sometimes mothers feel distressed at this; therefore, a mother may hasten to lift her child up in her arms, yet he runs away from her; she wants to give him a hug, yet he wants to be alone. Here, the child begins understanding that he is distinct from his mother.

This stage is very necessary for the child, and there are mothers who do not permit their children to traverse this stage; therefore, when the child grows up and gets married, he maintains an unhealthy[64] relationship with his mother. This stage is supposed to end when [the child] reaches the age of ten months, and at this age the child realizes that he and his mother are not the same person.

---

64   Literally: unsound.

2. The Rebellion Stage

It begins at the tenth month to the eighteenth month of age. So the child begins exercising his freedom; he can, and imagines that he can, do everything on his own. He may play with electricity, for example, or yank a cat's tail, or make a dart for the stairs if the door is opened... etc.

There is a difference between the first and second stages. In the first stage, the child knows that he is distinct from his mother, but he still depends on her. In the second stage, however, the child knows that he is distinct from his mother, and thinks that he can do everything on his own. There are people who remain all their life in the first stage, and do not move forward to the second stage. Likewise, there are people who remain all their life in the second stage, and think that they can do everything, being unaware of their limitedness. This is what Solomon the wise said, "And saw among the simple, I perceived among the youths, a young man devoid of understanding."[65]

In the second stage, here comes the role of the parents, that is to teach their child his limitedness, but without going to extremes in the treatment, because there are some parents who completely prohibit their children from playing, and want their child to stay still, and to sit still quietly, as though he were twenty or thirty years old. Such parents

---

65   Proverbs 7:7.

are dominating, and consequently, the child's personality turns out to be deficient or rebellious.

[On the contrary], there are parents who let their children play nonstop, or play whenever they want to, and sleep whenever they wish to. There is no discipline or control, and this is undoubtedly wrong. The child has to learn that there is a particular time for playing, a particular time for eating, and a particular time for sleeping, and also he has to keep everything intact, without destroying [anything]; otherwise, he will be met with certain consequences. For if children were left without rules to keep them in check, they become spoiled[66], who do not bear any responsibility.

3. The Getting Close and Friendliness Stage

This begins at the age of a year and a half to three years, in which the child realizes his limitedness, that he cannot do everything [on his own] but needs his parents. Therefore, he gets closer to them once again, and forms a relationship with his father and mother, but this relationship is characterized by a degree of maturity. It is different from the first relationship which had no clear distinction between the child and the mother.

This scenario recurs in multiple stages [of life]. For example, when the child reaches the age for

---

66 Literally: spoiled personalities.

entering school, separation become difficult and he might cry, but when he integrates into school, he does not ask about his mother or father [any longer]. Then he learns that he needs his father and mother.

In adolescence also, when the child matures, he wants to feel in himself that he has grown up, and many parents feel that they may lose control over the child, and consequently, they do not give him an opportunity for separation, even though this hinders his growth. The child [then] cannot take decisions on his own though he may be advanced in age, because the parents did not help in this. The reason in [them doing] this may be their selfishness, because the child's attachment to them gives them a sort of satisfaction.

It is important that the parents help their child separate from them, on the condition that they keep their eyes on him from a distance. Also they have to teach him how to make sound decisions on his own. For example, if a child, who is in high school, asks his father, "Should I go to medical school or engineering?" the father should not go ahead and say, "Medical school." Rather, he should begin by asking questions that lead his son to reach the right decision on his own. After this, the child will communicate with his father on another level, that is, a mature level, not the level of a child with his father, but the level of a mature young man with his father.

In the third stage, the child gets closer to his parents, without losing his sense of self. He has reached maturity. Sometimes the child uses some ways to build boundaries, and I have to help him do so using sound ways. For example, a mother turns off the television, so the child begins screaming loudly. This is his way of expressing that his mother has overstepped his boundaries.

Also, a mother may wake her children up to go to church. She picks a dress for her daughter and asks her to wear it, but the daughter may want another dress. If the mother had a controlling personality, she would insist that her daughter wear the dress she picked for her, and might get irritated and yell at her daughter, although the mother is supposed to encourage her daughter and approve the dress her daughter picked. Nevertheless, if the daughter picked an inappropriate dress, she should calmly explain to her why she does not approve of the dress.

The parents should encourage their children to say "No," and to accept to be at odds with them, and to let them express their opinions and make their decisions on their own. The girl, who does not know how to choose a dress for herself to wear at the age of four or five, will not know in the future how to choose a man to marry, because she has gotten used to there being another person making decisions for her.

There is a general remark we would like to make:

we do not know how to express our hurt feelings. If someone oversteps my boundaries, I get angry and do not speak, or I may yell and get irritated. Sadly, such reactions the children learn and they continue with them [in life]. If everyone obeys a father and [tries to] appease him if he gets angry, the son too will learn that when he gets angry and enraged, everyone will hasten to appease him. We have to teach our children how to express their anger in a sound way, and this teaching is done by being role models [ourselves]; therefore, our teacher Paul says, "Be angry, and do not sin."[67] It is a right for every person to express what is distressing him. For example, he may say, "I do not agree with this," or "This word hurt me," but he does not have the right to express it in a wrong way. When the Lord Christ, for example, was troubled that the disciples did not keep watch with Him in the Garden of Gethsemane, He did not contend with them, nor did he get angry or enraged, but on the contrary, He said to them, "What! Could you not watch with Me one hour?"[68] This makes it clear that the Lord Christ, when He became like us in everything as pertains to the flesh, did speak about His need, and did not follow the way of the avoider, because He had asked them to watch with him, and after that He made it clear to them that He knew that they loved Him, saying,

---

67   Ephesians 4:26.
68   Matthew 26:40.

"The spirit indeed is willing, but the flesh is weak."[69] He said the truth to them but with love.

The child has to feel safe as he says "No," and we have to encourage him when he says "No" to what is wrong, and have to teach him to accept the word "No" from others. If the child asks his parents to buy him a toy, but they refuse, he should not get enraged and angry. He has to learn that as it is his right to say "No," so he too has to accept the word "No" from others.

✝ ✝ ✝

---

69   Matthew 26:41.

3

Obstacles to Building
Boundaries

1. Emotional Withdrawal

A child may say "No" to his father, for example; then the mother would blame him for saying "No" to his father. It may also happen that the father may shun his child, and stop talking to him for three days, for example, and by so doing he is withdrawing emotionally from the relationship. So, the child feels that he has been deprived of love. Therefore, he cannot say "No" again, because he needs this love. Also, if he cannot say "No" again, consequently, he will not say it to [both] the good and the bad.

2. Aggression Against Boundaries

A mother, for example, may say to her daughter, "You should do such, or else you will be met with so-and-so consequences!" In the example we mentioned previously, if the girl refuses to wear the dress her mother picked, wanting to wear another dress [instead], the mother may say to her, "You have to wear the dress, or else you will be met with so-and-so consequences!" The girl, here, is afraid and cannot say "No" even when she grows up.

3. Being Excessively Controlling

Some parents think that they have to control their children because they love them, and consequently, they do not give them the freedom to speak or act. They also think that the best way to protect their children is by keeping them confined with themselves[70]. The Lord Christ—to Him be all glory—did not do this with us, however; He did not keep us confined in churches, without leaving them. Rather, He prayed, saying, "I do not pray that You should take them out of the world, but that You should keep them from the evil one."[71] Parents should not lock their children up, not allowing them to go out and go to certain places; instead, they should teach them how to protect themselves

---

70   i.e. keeping the children with their parents at all time.
71   John 17:15.

from the evil outside.

Sometimes it may happen that when a father sees a young man talking with his daughter in church, he quickly calls the priest and asks him, saying, "Please tell this young man to stay away from my daughter." If the priest, however, asked this young man to stay away from this girl, and he consents, what would the girl do with her [male] colleague in school or her [male] neighbor... etc.? Therefore, I have to teach my daughter how to say "No," that she may protect herself from evil.

Also, parents, often, take refuge in the bishop at church, so that he may execute for them what they want of their son, and they say to him, "Please, Your Grace, talk to our son, or sit with him." It even happens sometimes that the parents drag the son by force, so as to sit with the bishop, so the child feels distressed, for being forced to this. If this happened with me, personally, the first word I would give the child is, "Do you want, my beloved, to sit with me or not? This is your right," because if he sat with me forcedly, he would not listen to me attentively.

The Lord Christ did not impose anything on people by force. It happened one time that He sent messengers before His face, so they went and entered a village of the Samaritans, to prepare for Him, but they did not receive Him and shut their door in His face. So the disciples grew angry: "And when His disciples James and John saw this, they said, 'Lord, do You want us to command fire to come down from heaven and consume them, just as Elijah did?'"[72] But the Lord answered them [with a] "No," because that indicates a lack of respect for the freedom of others.

4. The Lack of Boundaries, and Indulgence

One of the obstacles of building boundaries is that the parents excessively spoil their children, fulfilling all their wishes. A father may think that the ideal fatherhood is to give his children everything they ask for. But in reality the world will not give us everything, and when the child realizes this, he becomes shocked and does not know how to deal with the world; therefore, most children, when they go out into the world, fail academically and scholastically.

And when he occupies a certain job, he works in it for a period [of time], then quits to move to another job. The reason is that he has not gotten used to hearing the word "No." When his manager says to him "No," he gets angry and quits the job, and he goes into another job. Then he quits this too, because his manager said "No" to him for something. Eventually, he ends up staying at home, having no work, because he has not gotten used to accepting the word "No" from others.

---

72   Luke 9:54.

5. The Flip-floppy (Unstable) Boundaries

One day, a father is unyielding; another day he is kind and very easygoing. Consequently, the child does not know how to behave or act; he becomes confused, not knowing when to say "No." Sometimes he feels safe towards his father and mother, so he talks and reveals whatever is in his heart, and the siting is exceedingly wonderful and enjoyable. Then a week later, the father and mother treat him with extreme harshness, holding him accountable for every word [he says]. Consequently, he does not feel a stability in the relationship, and this thing distresses him very much.

6. Getting Hurt Repeatedly

[Another] obstacle to building boundaries is that a person has suffered much hurt in his life, especially if they befell him unjustly. The matter may end up in the person believing that the world is unfair[73], and then, he has no control over his life, and everything is working against him, and thus, it is pointless to build boundaries.

In reality, we have no control over many of the matters conspiring against us, yet there is a sole freedom no one can take away from us; that is, the freedom to choose our reactions. What will, then, my reaction be, which I choose, if I am unjustly put

---

73   Literally: cannot be guaranteed.

into prison? Paul and Silas, when put unjustly into prison in Philippi, their reaction, which they chose, was to praise God: "But at midnight Paul and Silas were praying and singing hymns to God, and the prisoners were listening to them."[74] It is as though they were saying that God is present, so what else do we need besides. "Whom have I in heaven but You? And there is none upon earth that I desire besides You."[75]

And when there was an earthquake, and the doors of the prison were opened, they did not run away, because the prison doors were not what kept them confined inside the prison, and their reaction was to choose to remain in the prison. Therefore, when the keeper of the prison wanted to kill himself, "but Paul called with a loud voice, saying 'Do yourself no harm, for we are all here.'"[76] It is as though Paul wanted to say to him, "Do you think that the prison doors are what kept us confined? No, I, with my entire will, have consented to remain inside the prison; the prison could not take away joy from my heart."

Therefore, if a person chooses the right reactions, he will live happily, and will be able to build boundaries in his life. As for the person who has reached to the conviction that he has no control over his life, he will not be able to build boundaries.

---

74   Acts 16:25.
75   Psalms 73:25.
76   Acts 16:28.

7. Personal Attributes

Each of us possesses characteristics in his personality as a result of upbringing, environment, education, and the influence of the society he was brought up in. These factors shape us in a particular way. For example, in certain societies, a girl grows up and is brought up on that she has no rights, and she accepts this, and consequently, she is not able to build boundaries for herself.

8. Sin

Finally, living in sin is one of the obstacles to building boundaries. As the Holy Scripture says, "How much less man, who is abominable and filthy, who drinks iniquity like water!"[77] It is difficult for such a person to build boundaries in his life. If there were a person who steals, thereby encroaching upon the other's boundaries, how could he build boundaries?

Building boundaries requires divine help and the work of the Holy Spirit; therefore, the person has to offer true repentance, so as to be able to build boundaries, because any sin he commits is a trespass upon the boundaries of others.

---

77   Job 15:16.

4

When to Say "Yes" & When to Say "No"

There are numerous questions that need answers, so that we may be able to distinguish between when we say "Yes" to a matter and when we say "No." Setting boundaries with another [person] does not indicate my refusal of him or my consent; rather, it is the clarification of the extent of my abilities which I can work with.

Is building boundaries considered selfishness?

In reality, building boundaries is not selfishness; rather, it helps me serve the other [person] in a better way. For example, if there were a priest who could not say "No," but answered [with a "Yes"] continually till he reached the point of exhaustion, when a person comes asking his advice in a particular situation, he would not be able to offer a perfect and profitable advice. On the contrary, the priest who preserves his time and his boundaries, who is consequently mentally at ease, if someone came to him asking for an advice, he could offer it as it should.

[Here is] another example. When we are travelling by plane, the flight attendant comes at the beginning of the flight and talks about a procedure which should be followed for safety. One of the instructions she gives, while holding an oxygen mask, is that if the passenger felt that the oxygen [level] is getting low on board, the masks would be released automatically, and the passenger would have to put it on in the way she demonstrates. So, if there were a passenger with his young child, would he put the mask on himself first, or on the child first? If we were thinking emotionally, we would think that he would put it on his young child first, to save him. But the attendants advise that he should put the mask on himself first, and then on his child. The reason behind this is that if he were busy putting the mask on his son first, and the oxygen level became lower, he might faint and the child would faint as well, and would not be able to help him. But if he were to put the mask on himself first, thereby maintaining the oxygen level for himself, then he could save his son, even if he felt sick[78] for a short

---

78   Literally: tired.

while.

This action is not out of selfishness, and this is exactly what Moses' father-in-law said when he saw him judging in all the issues of the children of Israel who stood before him in long queues:

> So Moses' father-in-law said to him, "The thing that you do is not good. Both you and these people who are with you will surely wear yourselves out. For this thing is too much for you; you are not able to perform it by yourself. Listen now to my voice; I will give you counsel, and God will be with you: Stand before God for the people, so that you may bring the difficulties to God. And you shall teach them the statutes and the laws, and show them the way in which they must walk and the work they must do. Moreover you shall select from all the people able men, such as fear God, men of truth, hating covetousness; and place such over them to be rulers of thousands, rulers of hundreds, rulers of fifties, and rulers of tens. And let them judge the people at all times. Then it will be that every great matter they shall bring to you, but every small matter they themselves shall judge. So it will be easier for you, for they will bear the burden with you."[79]

---

79   Exodus 18:17–22.

Had Moses not followed his father-in-law's advice, he would have worn himself out, and all the people with him.

There is a difference, also, between selfishness and stewardship, because all of us are stewards. Selfishness is to focus on my own wishes and to satisfy them, while stewardship is to focus on my responsibilities. So I may say "No," so as to have time for my responsibilities, and by doing so, I am become a wise and faithful steward. Therefore, every person has to examine the reason for which he says "No." If a clerk were in his office, and someone came to him to complete a particular job, yet he said to him, "No, come tomorrow," this action would be [considered] selfish, because he did not perform his responsibility. But if he said to him, "You may sit here, for I have a lot of work to do," he is not selfish in this case.

Likewise, we have to distinguish between a wish and a need, for God gives us all that we need, but does not fulfill all our wishes. A person might wish to be wealthy, but God is obligated to satisfy all his needs which he admits, but not answering such a wish. As our teacher Paul the Apostle said, "Not that I speak in regard to need, for I have learned in whatever state I am, to be content."[80] The Apostle has reached the stage of contentment, because God has satisfied his needs, and not his wishes. The

---

80   Philippians 4:11.

needs are of the person's responsibilities. For the need for rest is not a sin, because if he does not get a sufficient amount of rest, he will not be able to complete the work required of him. For the sake of this God said:

> Six days you shall labor and do all your work, but the seventh day is the Sabbath of the LORD your God. In it you shall do no work: you, nor your son, nor your daughter, nor your male servant, nor your female servant, nor your ox, nor your donkey, nor any of your cattle, nor your stranger who is within your gates, that your male servant and your female servant may rest as well as you.[81]

And God has given us Himself as an example, "And on the seventh day God ended His work which He had done, and He rested on the seventh day from all His work which He had done."[82]

God, who has created in us this need, is obligated to fulfill it. For if I am working seven days [a week], I am not following the commandment, because I need to rest.

The matter is so, also, regarding the need for relationships and love. It is true that the Lord said, "and there are eunuchs who have made themselves

---

81   Deuteronomy 5:13–14.

82   Genesis 2:2.

eunuchs for the kingdom of heaven's sake. He who is able to accept it, let him accept it,"[83] but this choice is by the person's free will. The human being's natural need, however, is to be in a relationship with another person, and to grow in this relationship with him. God has given us these needs, and He satisfies them [Himself], but regarding our wishes, he says "No" to us, because He does not spoil us.

Let us think about salvation, for example. We all need salvation, and my responsibility is to accept the salvation which Christ accomplished for my sake on the cross. As our teacher Paul says, "Therefore, my beloved, as you have always obeyed, not as in my presence only, but now much more in my absence, work out your own salvation with fear and trembling."[84] The faithful and wise steward is he who is committed in all his responsibilities, including his needs, and he should satisfy these needs in a sound way.

Is every "No" a disobedience and rebellion?

As we have previously mentioned, when boundaries are weak, obedience is superficial, while the heart remains disobedient. The superficial obedience is lying, for the person here is lying to himself and lying to others. When we obey because of our inability to say "No," our obedience will not be

---

83   Matthew 19:12.

84   Philippians 2:12.

acceptable before God, because there exists rebellion and disobedience within [us]. But when we say "No" to what is good or to doing our responsibilities, this is disobedience of God's commandment, and loss of many opportunities for our growth and our good.

Is it likely that I would expose myself to harm due to building boundaries?

In reality, we cannot control the reaction of others in the process of building boundaries with them. Boundaries, however, will show us these who love us truly, and these who hate us, these who love the truth and these who hate it. The Lord Christ said the truth to the rich young man: "Jesus said to him, 'If you want to be perfect, go, sell what you have and give to the poor, and you will have treasure in heaven; and come, follow Me.'"[85] [He said this to him] though the Lord Christ, by His foreknowledge, knew that the rich young man would go away sorrowful. And undoubtedly this reaction may have troubled the Lord Christ "who desires all men to be saved and to come to the knowledge of the truth."[86] The Lord Christ, undoubtedly, was not happy that this young man went away sorrowful, yet, despite this, He said the truth to him.

We may be harmed or our feelings may be hurt, but we have to be truthful in love. We have

85   Matthew 19:21.

86   1 Timothy 2:4.

previously spoken about how to deal with the reactions of others; therefore, the role of supporting groups is very important here, because we cannot build boundaries with others, without being rooted and grounded in love[87].

Would I hurt the feelings of others when I set my boundaries?

We would like to say, at the start, that boundaries are not a means for offense, but are a protection and defense of self, exactly, in this, like a fence. We do not cause harm to others by building a fence for [our] land. I explain to others that these are my abilities, but those are not my abilities. The sensible[88] person will not be hurt because of boundaries, but will respect them; they may make him feel uncomfortable, but he will respect them.

The moderate person has many relationships, and does not depend on a single person to fulfil all of his needs of love and friendship. If this person's[89] circumstances change, he may become troubled, because he depends on this [one] person completely. The more relationships a person has, the more accepting he becomes of the boundaries of others. Therefore, we have to have many mature and sound relationships.

---

87 See Ephesians 3:17.

88 Literally: sound.

89 i.e. the one who depends on one person.

If I said "No" to my responsibilities towards others, is this an improper use of boundaries?

Here we have to speak briefly about the relationship between building boundaries and anger, especially concerning the compliant person who is a victim of being controlled. For this person may feel, after a while, that he is a victim of abuse and control, and thereby he becomes irascible, because he is not accustomed to saying "No." Therefore, the first time wherein he says "No," he may say it with hot anger, because this anger has been latent within him, and it [just] began to show. It is important that the person deals with this anger in a sound way. For example, if this person were not accustomed to building boundaries, and began building them, there would be no problem in him offering an apology about his anger, and not about building the boundaries.

An example of this is that if there were a wife who is always a compliant, not out of true obedience, but out of rebellion, then she wanted to build boundaries for herself. Her husband told her not to give tithes, but she said, "No, 'we ought to obey God rather than men.'[90]" She wanted to build boundaries with her husband, but she was afraid, and to shield herself from fear, she yelled at her husband, saying, "For many years [now] you have told me not to give my tithes. But I am no longer continuing in

---

90   Acts 5:29.

this thing; I am not listening to you." This took place because she has not learned how to express her opinion in a sound way. And because anger is not of her qualities, she offers apologies for what came out of her mouth. Here she is apologizing for the way in which she spoke, but she is committed to giving tithes, that is, to building boundaries.

Is it possible for me to get hurt if others set boundaries with me?

Usually I get hurt if others say to me "No," and [this is] for many reasons. It may be because of memories of childhood, so I feel the hardness [of the answer]. The reason may also be that I feel that who I am is derived from this person, and not from God, and then I may get hurt and may be much troubled when he says "No" to me. And perhaps, I may also be a dominating person; therefore, I feel unhappy when another person builds boundaries with me. And I may be a person who does not bear responsibility, so I feel distressed when someone builds boundaries with me, as we have previously spoken about the spoiled person.

We have to distinguish between being uncomfortable with the word "No" and not accepting it. We all, with no exception, do not feel comfortable when someone says "No" to us, and this is a normal thing. There is a difference, however, between a person who does not feel comfortable and another person who does not accept and rejects the word "No."

Not accepting leads this person to make desperate attempts so as to reach his goal, that is, to make the other [person] agree to what he is saying or what he is asking. These desperate attempts are different from those made by a person in defense of the truth.

Do boundaries generate the feeling of guilt?

Of the examples that make the intention of this question clear is that [when] there is a family wanting to settle in a new town, there may be people of the inhabitants of this town who offer them numerous services. They may go with them to look for a place to live in, and for a job; they offer them work, completing their paperwork. They help them out of indebtedness, so that this family may become their follower and a member of their party. They think that this favor[91] they [that is, the family] have to pay off when they are asked.

When this family, however, wants to build boundaries for themselves in this town, the [other] family that helped them will say to them, "After all this love and service, you do this to us?" Consequently, they feel guilty, and then they do not know whether to say "Yes" or "No."

---

91   Literally: debt.

The question here is: "Was this help a gift or a debt?" There is a difference between a gift and a debt: the gift [means] that I give without expecting anything in return, but the debt [means] that I give and expect the other person to pay back this giving. The gift is compensated by the feeling of appreciation, but the debt is compensated by doing something [in return], and not merely a word of thanks.

This also applies to salvation which the Lord Christ gave us; it is a gift, and therefore we feel appreciative toward God, and we endeavor to call others so that they may enjoy the salvation of Christ and may taste the love we ourselves have tasted.

The question we put forward here is that if I were in place of the family offering services, would I give as a gift or a debt? Would I give that I may take [back], or give while not expecting anything in return?

Would boundaries destroy my relationships?

Boundaries are not a sealed prison, but a fence whose doors can be opened and shut. If I have the feeling that I am applying boundaries in an improper way, I ought to open the doors once again, because boundaries preserve relationships, and not destroy them. Therefore, you have to own the boundaries, and do not permit the boundaries own you.

Boundaries destroy the mistakes [that are] in the relationship themselves, and there are two examples in Holy Scriptures that make this matter clear. The first [example] concerns the people of Nineveh. God set for them a boundary[92], that is: "And Jonah began to enter the city on the first day's walk. Then he cried out and said, 'Yet forty days, and Nineveh shall be overthrown!'"[93] The people of Nineveh, then, offered repentance, so God was reconciled with them. Boundaries are a protection for relationships.

The second example is about the relationship between St. Mark and Paul the Apostle. It so happened in the first missionary journey that St. Mark departed from Paul and Barnabas in Pamphylia and did not go with them to the work. Paul the Apostle did not like this behavior; therefore, when the second missionary journey began, Paul the Apostle refused that they take Mark with them:

> Now Barnabas was determined to take with them John called Mark. But Paul insisted that they should not take with them the one who had departed from them in Pamphylia, and had not gone with them to the work. Then the contention became so sharp that they parted from one another.[94]

---

92   Or: a limit.

93   Jonah 3:4.

94   Acts 15:37–39.

The question here is: did building boundaries here destroy the relationship between Mark and Paul? No, [it did not], because Paul the Apostle says to Timothy later on, "Only Luke is with me. Get Mark and bring him with you, for he is useful to me for ministry."[95]

Yes, there are boundaries, yet they did not destroy the relationships.

And glory be to our God, forever. Amen.

---

95   2 Timothy 4:11.